Internet DOs & DON'Ts

Don't Talk to Strangers Online

Shannon Miller

PowerKiDS press.

New York

Published in 2014 by The Rosen Publishing Group, Inc.
29 East 21st Street, New York, NY 10010

First Edition

Editor: Jennifer Way
Book Design: Andrew Povolny

Photo Credits: Cover KidStock/Blend Images/Getty Images; p. 5 Christopher Futcher/The Agency Collection/Getty Images; p. 7 Elisabeth Schmitt/Flickr Select/Getty Images; p. 9 Lilly Dong/Botanica/ Getty Images; p. 11 Eternity in an Instant/Workbook/Getty Images; p. 13 JGI/Jamie Grill/Blend Images/ Getty Images; p. 15 Cavan Images/Photodisc/Getty Images; p. 17 Apple Tree House/Digital Vision/Getty Images; p. 19 MIXA/Getty Images; p. 21 Rob Marmion/Shutterstock.com; p. 23 Tim Hawley/Stockbyte/ Getty Images.

Library of Congress Cataloging-in-Publication Data

Miller, Shannon.
 Don't talk to strangers online / by Shannon Miller. — First edition.
     pages cm. — (Internet dos & don'ts)
Includes index.
ISBN 978-1-4777-0755-5 (library binding) — ISBN 978-1-4777-1564-2 (pbk.) —
ISBN 978-1-4777-1565-9 (6-pack)
1. Internet and children—Juvenile literature. 2. Internet users—Juvenile literature. 3. Online sexual predators—Juvenile literature. 4. Safety education—Juvenile literature. I. Title.
HQ784.I58M555 2014
025.04028'9—dc23
                                          2013000214

Manufactured in the United States of America

CPSIA Compliance Information: Batch #S13PK4: For Further Information contact Rosen Publishing, New York, New York at 1-800-237-9932

Contents

Using the **Internet** is fun. You need to learn about online safety. This book will help you be safe online.

5

Websites may ask questions when you **log in**. They might do this before you play a game.

A website can **chat** with you. It may ask your age. It may need this fact to work.

9

Show a parent or teacher if a website asks you questions. She can see if the site is safe.

Parents and teachers know safe sites. They can find good sites for you. Some sites are only for kids.

13

You can chat with friends online. Never talk to **strangers** online! There are many reasons why.

15

A stranger may want to chat with you online. A stranger is anyone you do not know. Do not chat with strangers! It is not safe.

17

A stranger you chat with could bother you. He could find out where you live. That would be scary!

19

Tell a trusted adult if a stranger talks to you online. She wants you to be safe. She will know what to do.

Only talk to people that you know online. Never talk to strangers online. That is an Internet don't.

WORDS TO KNOW

Internet (IN-ter-net) A network that connects computers around the world. The Internet provides facts and information.

chat (CHAT) Using a computer to "talk" to another person.

log in (LOG IN) Giving a user name and a password to use a website.

strangers (STRAYN-jerz) People you do not know.

websites (WEB-syts) Places on the Internet.

INDEX

WEBSITES

Due to the changing nature of Internet links, PowerKids Press has developed an online list of websites related to the subject of this book. This site is updated regularly. Please use this link to access the list:
www.powerkidslinks.com/idd/talk/

3-14

ER025.04   Miller, Shannon
             Don't talk to strangers
         online.